# Independence for Latin America

## Contents

**T**he United States Leads the Way Why do we celebrate Independence Day on the Fourth of July? Well, that's when the original 13 colonies declared their independence from Great Britain in 1776. The signing of the Declaration of Independence led to a bloody five-year war between Great Britain and the colonies.

As you know, the colonies won that war and created the United States. What you may not know is that most of the other countries in North and South America were once colonies and also declared their independence from colonial masters. They too revolted and fought wars to become free. Many struggled to gain independence from Spain, but others declared independence from France or Portugal. Each of these countries has a national holiday when its citizens celebrate their independence, just as Americans do on the Fourth of July. This unit tells the story of these countries, located in a part of the world called Latin America, and how they won their freedom.

*Latin America includes Central and South America. It is called "Latin" America because the languages most widely spoken in the area are derived from Latin, the language of ancient Rome.*

### Why Did the Revolutions Happen?

Imagine what it would have been like to live in Latin America in the 1700s. Society was divided into rigid social classes, with Europeans having most of the power and native peoples and slaves having little or no power. People were born into a class, and for most of them, there was no way to move beyond that class. If you were a French **plantation** owner, you would have little to complain about, because you ran the show. And the same would have been true for a Spanish aristocrat who had been born in Spain and moved to one of the Spanish colonies in Latin America. But if you were a member of the lower classes, it was a different story.

Since the class system was very important in Latin America, let's begin by looking at the classes in Spanish America in the 1700s. In the Spanish colonies, the people considered to be the highest class had been born in Spain and then moved to the Americas. These people made up only a tiny percentage of the population, but they held most of the power, enjoyed special privileges, and controlled most of the wealth.

Creoles (KREE ohlz) were the next in line. Creoles were people who were born in America but whose parents or ancestors had been born in Spain. Some of the Creoles were rich and well-educated, but they were not trusted and seldom held important jobs in government. The Creoles were jealous of the Spaniards and angry because of the limitations Spaniards placed on them.

Below the Creoles were the Mestizos (mes TEE zohz), who were part Indian and part Spanish. Some of these people worked as craftspeople or shop owners. Others held minor jobs in the church or worked as managers in mines or on plantations. Few were rich, and few had much opportunity for improving their lives. Nevertheless, Mestizos had better lives than the Indians and slaves who occupied the classes below them.

> **vocabulary**
> **plantation** a large farm

In most colonies, Indians made up the great majority of the population. Some continued to live in the mountains, forests, and jungles. These rural Indians had little to do with the colonial society. But other Indians lived in missions founded by Spanish priests. These Indians worked as personal servants or as laborers on the plantations. Some also worked in the mines. Almost all of them were poor and had few rights. Occasionally, they would rise up, but their rebellions were ruthlessly put down.

Finally, there were the Africans. The Spanish had been bringing Africans to their American colonies as slaves since the early 1500s. Nevertheless, slavery was not widespread in the Spanish colonies. In 1800 there were only about 800,000 Africans in all of Spanish America, and most of these people lived on the islands of the Caribbean. In a few colonies the Africans may have been slightly better off than the Indians, but in most colonies they were the least powerful and the most oppressed group.

The lower three classes made up the vast majority of people living in Spanish America. If you belonged to one of these classes, you were almost certainly poor. You would have had few rights. You would have had little chance to get an education. Worst of all, there was little hope that things would ever change for you, your children, or your grandchildren.

The details of the class system varied from colony to colony. French and Portuguese colonies differed from Spanish colonies, and Spanish colonies differed from each other. However, the general situation was much the same all over Latin America: The Europeans were on top and the Indians and Africans, on the bottom.

## Foreign Influences

Now imagine how the people of Spanish America felt when they heard the ideas of John Locke, Voltaire, and the other writers of the Enlightenment. What would they have thought when they learned of the successful American Revolution? This revolution gave the people of the United States independence, freedom, justice, and opportunities that most people in Latin America could not even imagine.

And then there was the French Revolution, which broke out in 1789. Here was another case where the people rose up against their rulers and demanded rights. The people of Latin America saw these events and drew inspiration from them. They began to demand their own rights.

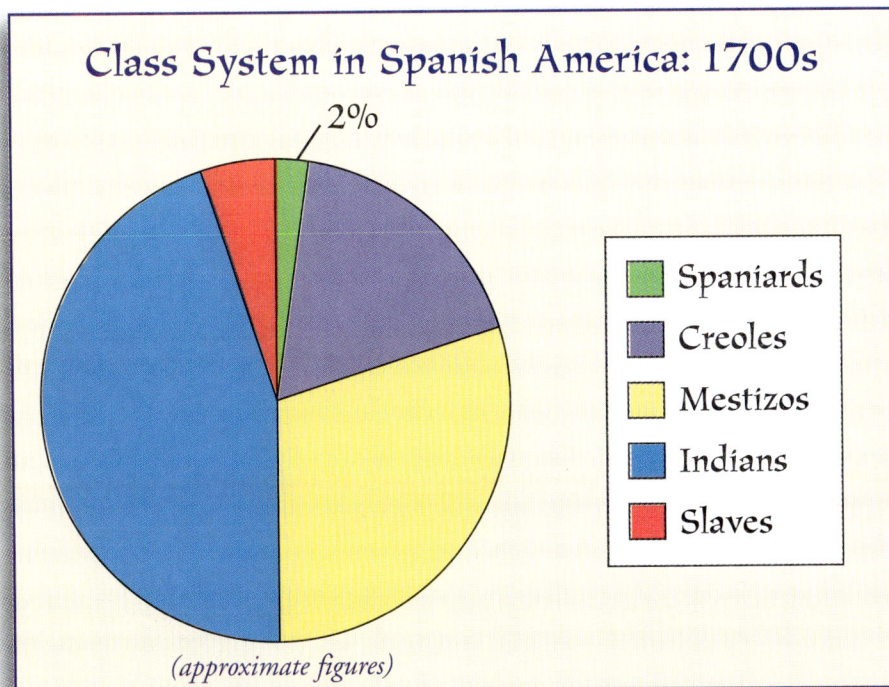

### Class System in Spanish America: 1700s

2%

- Spaniards
- Creoles
- Mestizos
- Indians
- Slaves

*(approximate figures)*

As the pie graph shows, Spaniards made up the smallest percentage of people living in Spanish America during the 1700s. Yet, this small percentage of people had a great deal of influence over the rest of the population, which included Creoles, Mestizos, Indians, and slaves.

Events in France influenced the Latin American independence movement in another way, too. In 1799 the revolutionary military leader Napoleon Bonaparte (BOH nuh pahrt) came to power in France. By 1808 he controlled Italy, Holland, part of Germany, and many European territories. In that year he invaded Spain and Portugal. Napoleon removed the Spanish king and put his brother Joseph Bonaparte on the Spanish throne. This event had an unusual result. It allowed the Spanish colonies in America to declare independence from Spain without having to be disloyal to their deposed Spanish king.

Revolution broke out throughout Spain's American colonies in 1810. It usually began within the local governments in each colony. These governments were in the hands of **cabildos** (kuh BIHL dohz), or city councils.

These city councils decided the time was right to proclaim their independence from Spain. Caracas, the capital of Venezuela, started the revolution in April 1810. Buenos Aires, the capital of La Plata, which includes modern Argentina, Uruguay, Paraguay, and Bolivia, followed in May. Next came Bogotá, the capital of New Grenada, in July. Quito, which became the capital of Ecuador, rebelled in August, and Santiago, the capital of Chile, joined the revolutionary movement in September. The big exception to this trend of city councils leading the fight for independence was in Mexico, where a Creole priest named Miguel Hidalgo y Costilla (mee GEL hih DAL goh ee kohs TEE yah) started Mexico's fight for independence in September 1810.

## Colonies in the Americas, 1700

| | |
|---|---|
| ⬛ | English colonies |
| 🟩 | French colonies |
| ⬜ | Spanish colonies |
| 🟧 | Portuguese colonies |
| 🟨 | Dutch colonies |

0     750     1,500 miles
0   750   1,500 kilometers

*Spanish, Portuguese, French, English, and Dutch colonies had been established in the Americas by 1700.*

### vocabulary
**cabildo** the government of a city in Latin America; the city council

The people you will learn about in this unit, like Toussaint L'Ouverture (too SAN loo ver TOOR) of Haiti, Simón Bolívar (see MAWN boh LEE vahr) of Venezuela, and José de San Martín (hoh SAY de sahn mahr TEEN) of Argentina, wanted to create governments based on the same principles as those of the United States government. Many of these leaders had been to the United States. They wanted governments that would give the people of Latin America those same rights of freedom, justice, and opportunity. And they believed that revolution was the only way to get what they wanted.

**The Night of Fire** It was August 1791. The sound of drums echoed from mountain to mountain and across the plain. French plantation owners in Haiti heard the dim sound of the drum beats in the distance but were not worried. They had heard them before.

It was no secret that escaped slaves, called *maroons* (muh ROONZ), hid out in the mountains. There they practiced their ancient African religion. The slaves called this religion *voodoo*.

The drums really were celebrating a voodoo rite, but it was not the usual ceremony the planters thought it was. The slaves were plotting a rebellion!

Deep in the mountains a slave and voodoo priest named Boukman led the ceremony. Around him were gathered the leaders of the slaves from across the Plain du Nord (plen duh nor), the northern plain of Haiti. Haiti was a French colony in the Caribbean, on the island of Hispaniola (hihs pun YOH luh).

*This painting shows a voodoo ceremony. Voodoo was a powerful force on the island of Hispaniola in the early 1800s.*

Boukman was not a field hand like most slaves. He had been a foreman who ran field crews. Later, he worked his way up to being a coachman. That was an important job on a plantation. Moreover, Boukman was a huge man who commanded respect through size alone.

All eyes followed Boukman as he gave his instructions and inspired his followers to have courage. He promised them that if they died during the rebellion, they would wake up in Africa. He concluded with a song that ends, "Hearken unto Liberty, that speaks now in all our hearts."

One week later, on August 22, 1791, some 50,000 slaves rose up and swept across the Plain du Nord. Armed with **machetes** (muh SHET eez) and **scythes** (sythz), the slaves moved in an unstoppable wave across the land. They killed and tortured plantation owners and their families. They set fire to the houses and barns and even to the crops. The fires spread, covering the horizon and sweeping across fields, plantations, and forests. The night became as bright as day. The rich plantations were in ruins, and slave armies controlled the countryside.

**vocabulary**
**machete** a large, heavy knife used for cutting down sugarcane and brush
**scythe** a long, curving blade used for cutting grain and long grasses

Over the next few days, the slave army destroyed all the plantations on the Plain du Nord. Most of the surviving French took shelter in Cap François (frahn SWAH) the capital of the province.

The night on which the rebellion began became known as the Night of Fire. It marked the beginning of a 13-year struggle to create Haiti, the first black republic in the world and the first independent state in Latin America.

## Haiti in 1791

Before we go further, you need to know something about Haiti prior to August 1791, when the revolution began. Haiti was a French colony called St. Domingue (san duh MANG), and it was the richest colony in the Caribbean. A century earlier, French planters had taken over the western third of the island of Hispaniola from the Spanish.

During the eighteenth century, thousands of African slaves were captured from their villages and brought in chains to North and South America and the Caribbean. Many of those slaves were taken to St. Domingue. There, they were put to work clearing the forests and planting crops of sugar, coffee, cotton, and indigo. Indigo is a plant that produces a deep blue dye. It was in demand to dye cotton cloth made in England.

The crops the slaves planted were sold in Europe, where demand for sugar, coffee, cotton, and dyes made the prices high. The French landowners became wealthy beyond their wildest dreams. Of course, the more money they made, the more land they cleared, and the more slaves they wanted.

About 700,000 slaves worked to produce the crops that made the French landowners rich. The French population of about 35,000 included landowners, plantation managers and supervisors, colonial officials, soldiers, priests, nuns, and shopkeepers. In addition, there were some 40,000 *mulattos*. Mulattos were people of mixed race—usually with white French fathers and black slave mothers.

For every French person in the colony, there were about 20 slaves. With so many more slaves than French people, you might think that rebellion was a constant threat. But the French were not worried. They didn't think the slaves could carry out a successful uprising. Besides that, the French controlled all the guns. Against the well-armed and highly trained French soldiers, slaves

*Slaves in pre-revolutionary Haiti (St. Domingue) worked under harsh conditions on the many plantations there.*

would have no chance. At least, that's what the French thought.

## The Struggle Continues

Boukman's uprising and the Night of Fire shocked the French, but they soon fought back. The French soldiers were well armed and trained. And if the slaves had been brutal and savage in their rebellion, the French were even worse in seeking revenge. Thousands of slaves were killed. The rest were chased into hiding in the mountains. Soon, northern St. Domingue was divided into two parts. The rebellious slaves controlled the mountains, and the French soldiers held the coastal towns, where the planters and French officials had fled during the uprising.

The uprising spread to the western part of the island. There, the planters found out what had happened in the north and put up more resistance. Port-au-Prince, the capital of the west, was saved, and the rebellion was largely controlled.

Meanwhile, in the north, Boukman was killed in battle. He was replaced by two other ex-slaves, Biassou (bee ah SOO) and Jean François (zhahn frahn SWAH). They proved to be poor leaders. Would the revolution become just a failed slave uprising?

## Toussaint L'Ouverture

A new leader emerged out of the confusion. His name was François Dominique Toussaint. Later he added L'Ouverture at the end of his name. He is usually known as Toussaint L'Ouverture. *L'Ouverture* means "the opening" in French. It is said that Toussaint's enemies gave him that name because he could always find an opening in their defense to attack them.

Toussaint was born in 1743 on a plantation in northern St. Domingue. There is a legend that

Toussaint's father was an African chief who was captured and made a slave. No one knows for sure if this is true. However, Toussaint's father did teach him that there is power in knowledge. His stepfather, a priest, helped Toussaint gain that power. He taught Toussaint how to read and write French and Latin and how to use herbs and plants for healing.

Toussaint was not among the slaves who participated in the first hours of the Night of Fire. He certainly saw the fires from the plantation where he lived. And when the rebellion reached the plantation, his first concern was to get his wife and children to safety. Then Toussaint drove the family of the French manager of the plantation to safety. The manager had given Toussaint his freedom years before, and the former slave wanted to protect him and his family.

*Toussaint L'Ouverture was a great revolutionary leader in Haiti.*

Once he had taken care of his personal responsibilities, Toussaint enthusiastically joined in the revolution. "Those first moments," he later said, "were moments of beautiful delirium [dreaminess], born of a great love of freedom."

Because of his knowledge of healing, Toussaint's first service in the slave revolt was as a doctor. Soon, however, he was giving military advice as well as medical care. The slave army was ruthless and undisciplined. They destroyed everything in their path, including the crops. After the army passed through, there was nothing for the slaves to eat but whatever wild plants and animals they could find.

Toussaint urged the leaders to teach the troops discipline and to stop destroying the crops and other things they needed for themselves. Within a short time, Toussaint was made a commander of part of the army. He taught his soldiers discipline and trained them like a professional army.

## Toussaint Leads the Rebellion

Not only were Biassou and Jean François poor leaders, but they were disloyal to the cause of freedom as well. In December 1791, when it looked as if the French might succeed in putting down the revolt, Biassou and Jean François struck a deal to turn over the former slaves in return for their own freedom. Toussaint would have no part of this. Instead, he organized the slaves into a **guerrilla army** that attacked the French when they least expected it.

After each attack the guerrilla army would disappear back into the forests and mountains. There, they would wait until Toussaint found another opportunity for a surprise attack. He came at the French with amazing speed and from unexpected directions. The French could never catch him, and they could never relax. They never knew when or where Toussaint's army would appear.

Toussaint was a memorable figure as he rode before his troops. He was a superb horseman who chose to ride without a saddle. He dressed in the splendid uniform of a captured French officer, often with a handkerchief wrapped around his head. Under his coat there was an odd shape.

Some people thought Toussaint was hunchbacked. His troops knew better. The lump was actually a box filled with small knives and tweezers, herbs, salves, ointments, and other supplies. Besides leading his soldiers, he was ready to repair their wounds and ease their pains from battle injuries.

Toussaint won several victories over the French. He promised the French townspeople that he would treat them well if they surrendered. They trusted Toussaint, and so several towns did surrender to the rebels.

Of course, the slaves were fighting for their freedom. But no matter how many victories they won or how many towns surrendered, the French government refused to free the slaves.

While the slaves continued to fight for their freedom against the French in St. Domingue, Spain and Great Britain were also at war with

**vocabulary**

**guerrilla army** a group of soldiers who usually are volunteers and not highly trained, professional soldiers

*This illustration shows Toussaint L'Ouverture, in the center with a red vest, leading his troops in a pitched battle during Haiti's revolution against the French.*

France. Toussaint believed the Spanish could help him win liberty. As a result, he joined the Spanish forces in Santo Domingo, the eastern part of Hispaniola. He was named a general and won battles for the Spanish. Still, he had been raised in a French colony and felt some loyalty to France.

In 1794, France passed a law freeing all slaves. When he heard about the French action, Toussaint switched sides and began fighting for France. Toussaint was made lieutenant governor, the second in command of the colony, and he succeeded in driving the Spanish troops from St. Domingue.

By 1795, Toussaint was the most important man in St. Domingue. He was worried that the economy of the island would collapse if he didn't do something—four years of revolution had destroyed most of the plantations and driven off the owners. He asked the former slaves to come back and work in the fields and the sugar mills. But now, the workers were free—they weren't whipped and they shared in the profits.

Slowly, Toussaint began to create a separate government in St. Domingue. A constitution was written. The constitution did not claim independence from France but did declare slavery to be forever ended. Toussaint negotiated treaties with Great Britain and the United States and began to trade sugar for arms.

In 1801, Toussaint became ruler of the entire island of Hispaniola in the name of France. All of Toussaint's plans were beginning to work out, or so it seemed. But Toussaint had not reckoned with Napoleon, who now ruled France.

## Napoleon's War

Napoleon was at the height of his power. He had conquered much of Europe and was carrying on a long war with Great Britain. Battles were fought around the world. To support his war, Napoleon needed the vast wealth that St. Domingue had once produced. He thought that the island's economy could only be restored by bringing back slavery. Napoleon organized an invasion of St. Domingue. It would be led by his brother-in-law, General Victor Leclerc. Leclerc had an army of 43,000 soldiers. It was the largest invasion force in the history of France.

Spies reported Napoleon's plans to Toussaint. A wise man, he was not surprised by the betrayal, but it caused him great sorrow. Toussaint had shown great loyalty to France, but Napoleon was not interested in the freedom of black people thousands of miles away. "I counted on this happening," Toussaint said. "I have known that they would come and that the reason behind it would be that one and only goal: reinstatement of slavery. However, we will never again submit to that."

Toussaint immediately began making preparations. He imported weapons from the United States. He reinforced his forts. He had pits and trenches dug in the forests for his soldiers. He drafted all young men 12 years old and over to train for his army.

Despite his preparations, Toussaint almost lost courage when he saw the French fleet. It is said that he cried: "Friends, we are doomed. All of France has come. Let us at least show ourselves worthy of our freedom."

As soon as the French army landed, bloodshed and violence returned. Toussaint ordered his army to burn everything rather than turn anything

over to the French. Entire cities burned. The fighting was intense. The French general Leclerc described the desperate rebels in a report to Napoleon: "These people here are beside themselves with fury. They never withdraw or give up. They sing as they are facing death and they still encourage each other while they are dying. They seem not to know pain. Send reinforcements!"

## Toussaint Captured

Leclerc knew the fight to take control of St. Domingue would be long and hard as long as Toussaint was leading the rebels. So Leclerc tricked Toussaint into meeting with one of his officers. Toussaint and his family were captured and put on a ship for France. As Toussaint stood on board the ship, he said: "In overthrowing me you have cut down in St. Domingue only the trunk of the tree of liberty. It will spring up again from the roots, for they are many and they are deep." Toussaint and his family were separated, and he was sent to a prison in the mountains near Switzerland.

Toussaint, who had spent his life on a tropical island, must have been miserable in the Swiss mountains. He was separated from his family and living in a cold, damp prison. Of course, there wouldn't have been any heat, even in the winter. The French didn't execute Toussaint because they knew that that would lead to more problems in St. Domingue. However, if the rebel leader died in prison, well, that was not their fault. They certainly weren't unhappy when Toussaint, who had been such a great leader of the Haitian people, caught pneumonia and died in 1803.

## France Loses St. Domingue

Back in St. Domingue, the French were having new problems. The ex-slaves weren't strong enough to fight the French army head on, but they continued their guerrilla war. The French killed thousands of black people, but this only made things worse. The more black people they killed, the greater became the resistance.

In this painting by Jacques-Louis David, Napoleon Bonaparte leads his troops across the Alps between France and Austria in 1800.

The main leader of the former slaves at this time was Jean Jacques Dessalines (zhahn  zhahk  day sa LEEN). He had been born in Africa and brought to St. Domingue as a slave. Unlike Toussaint, he had no loyalty to France. He wanted to do more than just end slavery. He wanted to make St. Domingue independent.

Dessalines continued Toussaint's policy of burning farms and towns rather than letting the French capture them. The resistance caused great problems for the French. Nevertheless, they had thousands of troops and far superior weapons. It was only a matter of time before they would regain control of St. Domingue. But, as it turned out, time was about to run out for the French.

## The Fall of the French

Yellow fever, a deadly disease carried by mosquitoes, began to spread through the French army. Thousands of French soldiers died. Reinforcements were sent, but they died, too. Even General Leclerc fell victim to the disease.

Finally, unable to conquer the epidemic, the remains of the French army left St. Domingue in 1803. Of the 43,000 men France had sent to the island, only 8,000 lived to sail back home.

Why didn't the blacks in St. Domingue suffer as much from yellow fever as the French? The answer is that they had lived with the disease longer. They had brought it to the island from Africa. The Africans caught yellow fever just like the Europeans. However, most Africans survived the disease while most Europeans died from it.

On January 1, 1804, Dessalines declared St. Domingue independent. He gave the country a new name, Haiti. That was the Indian name for the island of Hispaniola before Europeans settled there.

Haiti was in ruins. Thirteen years of war had destroyed towns and farms. Dessalines knew he would have to do something to rebuild. He told the people they would have to go back to the farms and work harder than they had when they were slaves. It was the only way.

Soon, Dessalines became a dictator. In October 1804 he proclaimed himself Emperor Jacques I. The economy began to get better, but the people didn't like being forced to work on the hated plantations. They were free, why should they work like slaves? In October 1806, two and a half years after he declared Haiti's independence, Dessalines was murdered.

Haiti never had another leader like Toussaint L'Ouverture. Instead, Dessalines was more typical of the men who would rule the country. Haiti has never recovered completely from the destruction of the battle for independence. For 200 years it has suffered under the rule of dictators and bad government. These conditions have made it one of the poorest countries in the world.

*This illustration shows Jean Jacques Dessalines riding at the head of some of his officers.*

# Mexico's Fight for Independence

**I**ndependence Day, 2001 It is late in the day of September 15. A crowd of people begins to gather in the Zócalo, the open plaza in the center of Mexico City. The crowd grows and grows. By ten o'clock that night, hundreds of thousands of Mexicans have assembled.

They are there to listen to the president of Mexico. He has an important message for them, one he wants them all to hear and to remember. Afterward, he will ring a great bell that hangs in the arch high above the main entrance to the National Palace.

Everywhere you look are red, white, and green—the national colors of Mexico. The National Palace is draped with red, white, and green cloth, and colored lights display a giant Mexican flag. Most of the people in the huge crowd are waving small Mexican flags.

This is the way that Mexicans begin the celebration of their independence from Spain. The president will remind everyone of the long struggle for independence and the sacrifices made by thousands of Mexicans. At eleven o'clock the president will ring Mexico's Liberty Bell and call out *Viva México!* ("Long live Mexico!"), and the crowd will answer back, *Viva México, Viva la independencia!* ("Long live Mexico! Long live independence!"). Almost 200 years ago on this day in 1810, the colony of Mexico was on the brink of a long struggle. The War for Independence began the next day, September 16, 1810.

## The Start of a Revolution

The revolution began with a group of men who called themselves the Literary and Social Club of Querétaro (kuh RAYT uh roh). In reality, it wasn't a social and literary society at all. The members were really plotting a revolution against Spain. Lots of Mexicans were unhappy with Spanish rule.

Indians were unhappy because they didn't have enough land. Many of them were forced to work on the big **haciendas** (hah see EN duhs), or farms, for little or no pay. They owed money to the landowners. The Indians couldn't leave the haciendas until their debts were paid. They never earned enough money, so they were trapped.

### vocabulary
**hacienda** a large ranch or plantation in Latin America
**padre** the Spanish word for "father"; a traditional form of address for a Roman Catholic priest

The mestizos, part Indian and part Spanish, were unhappy because they were poor and didn't have good jobs. Because the mestizos were of mixed descent, they were looked down on. They hoped they might get more respect and power if Mexico was independent. With more power they would also have more money.

The Creoles were unhappy because they were shut out of the most powerful positions in Mexico. Many landowners, professionals, and other important people were Creoles. They owned most of the haciendas. But the Spaniards held the real power in Mexico. If Creoles could get rid of these people, they would control Mexico's government.

**Padre** (PAH dray) Miguel Hidalgo y Castilla (mee GEL ee THAHL goh ee kahs TEE yah) was a leading member of the Literary and Social Club. Padre Hidalgo was a priest in the village of Dolores.

Hidalgo was a Creole who had lived for the first 12 years of his life on a hacienda where his father was manager. When he was 12, Hidalgo went away to school. He was very bright and determined to learn. Hidalgo spent the next 12 years studying. Then, he became a priest and a teacher. He held several important posts at the Catholic college in Valladolid (val uh doh LIHD). Eventually, he became the rector, or head, of the college. He did important work, was paid well, and was highly respected. His life was a success, but it was about to change.

You see, Hidalgo was becoming a bit of a troublemaker. He had begun to question authority; instead of teaching the traditional material, he was spending more and more time talking about ways to improve government. He also showed himself to be a poor manager of money. As rector, he put the college in debt by spending too much money on food and housing for students. The people in charge of the college were not happy with this unexpected debt. It should also be pointed out that Hidalgo had one or two other bad personal habits. For example, he liked to gamble.

No one knows which of these problems caught up with him. Maybe it was all of them. Maybe it was something else altogether. For some reason, though, Hidalgo was suddenly forced to quit his job at the college. He was sent to serve as a priest in a very small village.

## A Good Priest

Hidalgo spent ten years in this village before moving on to a somewhat larger church in Dolores. The people considered him a good priest who worked hard to improve their lives. In Dolores, he helped the Otomí Indians plant grapevines and mulberry trees. The Indian farmers could use the grapes to make wine, which they would sell. Also, the Indians could sell the silk thread from the cocoons of the silkworms that lived on the mulberry trees. There was only one problem: It was illegal for Indians to do these things. The Spaniards wanted to keep these profitable activities for themselves. Padre Hidalgo became a beloved figure in Dolores because he was willing to break the law in order to help the Indians. The people loved him because he wasn't afraid to break rules when he thought they were wrong.

When he went to Querétaro, Hidalgo would meet with his friends in the Literary and Social Club to talk about the problems of the country. One of his best friends was Ignacio Allende (eeg NAH syoh ah YAYN day), a captain and commander of the local army post. He was a Creole, like Padre Hidalgo, and he didn't like Spanish rule either. Juan Aldama (hwahn ahl DAH mah) was another military officer opposed to Spanish rule in Mexico. He was a good friend of Hidalgo and Allende.

*Padre Miguel Hidalgo y Castilla was one of Mexico's first revolutionary heroes.*

## Revolutionary Times

By 1810, Mexico had been under Spanish rule for almost 300 years. The injustices, inequality, and dissatisfaction that members of the Literary and Social Club discussed were not new. Why, then, did revolution finally break out at this time?

You will recall that events in Europe made this time especially ripe for revolution in Latin America. Napoleon, the ruler of France, had invaded Spain and overthrown the king. His brother Joseph Bonaparte now ruled there. Rebels like Hidalgo and Allende could claim that they were fighting against France, not Spain. Of course, they really wanted to make Mexico independent.

So the members of the Literary and Social Club plotted their revolution. They were men of conscience. They knew that the Spaniards had mistreated people. They wanted to improve people's lives. But to be honest, they also wanted more power for themselves. They were all Creoles, and they wanted to see the Creoles replace the Spaniards at the top of the Mexican social ladder.

The plotters in Querétaro had been planning for about a year—since the fall of 1809. By September 1810, the plans were almost complete. The date set for the uprising was October 2. Then something went wrong. The plot was discovered! Some members of the conspiracy had already been arrested. The government was searching for the rest. When the news reached Hidalgo, Allende, and Aldama on September 15, they were in Dolores. They had to decide what to do. Should they run? Should they start the revolution early? Some things had still not been done. If they began early, would the people rise up to support them?

While the others argued frantically over what to do, Hidalgo sat quietly. He had made his decision. During a pause in the debate, he declared, "In action everything is accomplished, we must not lose time; you will all see the oppressor's [tyrant's] yoke broken and beaten into the ground."

It was then nighttime on September 15. Padre Hidalgo ran to the church tower and began to ring the bell. The people of Dolores knew something important was about to happen. When a crowd had gathered in front of the church, Hidalgo told them it was time to take up arms. If they threw out the Spaniards, they would get land. They wouldn't have to work on the haciendas anymore. As his speech drew to an end, Hidalgo shouted, "Independence and Death to the Spaniards! Long live the Virgin of Guadalupe!" The Virgin of Guadalupe was an image of Mary, the mother of Jesus, that was especially important to Indians, who made up most of his audience.

These final words are called the *Grito de Dolores* ("Cry of Dolores"). They are repeated every year on the night of September 15 by the president of Mexico.

Hidalgo's speech inspired his listeners. They ran home to get whatever weapons they could find. Most of them had machetes that were used for farm work. Others grabbed hoes and other farm tools, sticks to use as clubs, or even stones to throw. By now it was the morning of September 16. Almost 800 men were gathered outside Hidalgo's house. They were the beginning of the revolutionary army.

## An Undisciplined Army

News of Padre Hidalgo's rebellion spread quickly to other villages. Soon the whole province was up in arms. The Indians saw their chance for revenge and they took it. Within just a few days, thousands of people had joined the revolution. Padre Hidalgo became the leader, and Ignacio Allende and Juan Aldama were his aides, or assistants. Within a week, 25,000 rebels had joined the army.

Hidalgo seemed an unlikely man to lead a revolutionary army. He was already 57 years old when the revolution began. He had no military experience, and he didn't appear to be a great national hero. He was of medium height with rounded shoulders and a dark complexion.

Hidalgo's green eyes were quick and lively, but his movements were slow and thoughtful. He let his head droop over his chest, and he was nearly bald, with just a little white hair. Hidalgo wore the simple clothing of a village priest. And yet, despite his appearance, the people of Mexico loved Hidalgo and confidently followed him as their revolutionary leader.

The army quickly captured several towns and villages. Then, on September 28, they attacked the rich mining city of Guanajuato (wahn uh HWAHT oh). The Spaniards had prepared for the attack by turning the strongest building in town, the Alhóndiga (ahl-OHN-dee-gah), into a fort. This huge grain storage building was big enough for all the leaders, the soldiers, the Spanish citizens, and other sympathizers.

The Spanish soldiers were well-trained and armed with guns and swords, but there were only a few hundred of them. They had no chance against the thousands of rebels that threw themselves into the attack. No matter how many were killed, the rebels kept coming. Soon they broke into the Alhóndiga. Hidalgo couldn't control the unruly troops, who fell quickly on the Spaniards. All but a few of the 500 Spaniards were killed. Nearly 2,000 of Hidalgo's rebels died, too.

The town was now defenseless and the rebels could not be controlled. The army looted the entire city, tore up homes and businesses, and destroyed mining equipment. Two days later, Hidalgo ordered the army to stop, but the order was ignored. The army had become a mob that laid waste to the city.

The army's lack of discipline was a great problem, and Hidalgo and the other leaders did not know how to solve it. Hidalgo, in fact, thought the rebels should be allowed to loot as a reward for joining the revolution. "We have no arms but theirs with which to defend ourselves," he said, "and if we begin to punish them, we shall not find them when we need them."

Whether it was a mob or an army, the rebels continued to win battles. And with every victory, more people joined the revolution. But Miguel Hidalgo was a priest, not a soldier. The victory in Guanajuato was won because there were few Spanish soldiers to defend the city. A large and well-prepared Spanish army would be a lot harder for the undisciplined rebel army to defeat. Ignacio Allende, who was a soldier, tried to warn Hidalgo of the danger. But the priest was convinced he could beat the Spaniards.

This painting by Diego Rivera, showing Mexico's many revolutions, is in Mexico City's National Palace. The white-haired figure in the center is Padre Hidalgo.

## The Revolution Stumbles

In October, Hidalgo began a march toward the capital, Mexico City. If he could capture the capital, it would end most of the Spanish resistance. However, as he advanced closer to the capital, Hidalgo discovered that not everyone supported his rebellion. Few people in this part of Mexico would join his army. Many, in fact, feared him and disliked the destruction that followed his army. In the end, Hidalgo decided not to attack Mexico City. Instead, he led the army west toward Guadalajara (gwah dul uh HAHR uh), an important city in western Mexico.

Meanwhile, the soldiers in his army began to leave. Army life turned out to be dull. To make matters worse, it was time to plant crops, and without corn to eat, the men didn't know how they and their families could survive. So the army dwindled. By the time Hidalgo reached Guadalajara, he had only about 7,000 soldiers left. He was, however, greeted like a hero; bands played as city leaders greeted him.

Hidalgo, Allende, and Aldama used the time in Guadalajara to gather more soldiers, to train their army, and to make cannons and other weapons. But the Spanish army was also preparing and soon marched on Guadalajara. The rebels went out to meet them.

Allende had feared that the rebel army would be no match for the trained Spanish troops, but the battle was evenly fought for six hours. Then a lucky shot from a Spanish cannon struck one of Hidalgo's ammunition wagons. A huge explosion occurred, and the dry grass of the battlefield caught fire. The rebel army became confused at first and then panicked and fled the battlefield. Hidalgo, Allende, and Aldama could do nothing but flee with their army.

The survivors fled north to the city of Saltillo, an old mining center. There, the rebels were lured into an ambush and captured. The leaders were tried and sentenced to death. Hidalgo was shot by a firing squad on July 31, 1811, less than a year after he began the revolution.

Hidalgo was a priest, not a soldier. He ultimately failed to win the revolution. Still, he is the main hero of Mexico's long struggle for independence. In the National Palace in Mexico City there are great **murals** painted by Diego Rivera, one of Mexico's most famous artists, that depict all of Mexican history. Padre Hidalgo and Ignacio Allende are among the great revolutionary leaders shown.

> **vocabulary**
> **mural** a large picture that is usually painted directly on the wall of a building

## José María Morelos

After the capture of Hidalgo, the rebel army broke up, but the revolution did not end. Instead, it was fought in small battles by bands of guerrilla soldiers. There were lots of leaders, but many were little more than bandits. One leader did stand out, though. He was José María Morelos (hoh SAY mah REE ah moh RAY lohs).

Morelos had been a friend of Hidalgo and had commanded an army fighting in southern Mexico while Hidalgo had been in the center. Morelos didn't think that the Mexicans could hope to win the revolution by fighting the Spaniards in open battle. That's why he used guerrilla tactics.

Morelos led a guerrilla war in southern Mexico for five years. He assembled a strong army of about 9,000 men. And unlike

*José Morelos continued Mexico's revolution against Spain after Hidalgo died.*

Hidalgo's army, Morelos's army was well disciplined and well equipped. Eventually, he controlled most of southern Mexico.

Morelos was different from Hidalgo in another important way. He had a specific plan for the revolution, while Hidalgo had just made vague promises. Morelos said the government should treat everyone—Indians, mestizos, and Creoles—equally. To make sure that Spaniards wouldn't gain control again, he wanted a law that would allow only people born in Mexico to hold government offices. These policies earned Morelos the loyalty of the Indians and mestizos.

But the most revolutionary thing of all that Morelos did was to say he would take the land away from the big hacienda owners and give it to the workers. The Creoles didn't like the idea of equality. They hated that Morelos had promised to break up the haciendas. After all, most of the haciendas were owned by Creoles.

So the Creoles didn't support Morelos. This was his downfall. After five years of fighting, he was captured on November 15, 1815. The Creoles could have sent an army to keep him from being captured by the Spaniards, but they didn't. Morelos was shot, just as Hidalgo had been. Two great heroes of the War for Independence had been killed, and the goal had not yet been attained.

### The Long Road to Victory

By the time of Morelos's death, the country had been at war for five years. People were suffering badly. Crops had failed because hacienda owners had been driven from their land or had run away. Many Indian farmers had left their land to fight. There were bandits everywhere. Many of them were soldiers who deserted the rebel army when things got bad. Roads were not kept up and businesses couldn't get products to sell.

In spite of everything, the war continued. The Spanish army wasn't strong enough to defeat the rebels, and the rebels never managed to build up enough power to defeat the government.

**Mexico's Independence from Spain, 1821**

Colorado R.
Red R.
Rio Grande
Gulf of Mexico
Saltillo
MEXICO
Guanajuato
Guadalajara
Mexico City
PACIFIC OCEAN

Mexico in 1821
Present-day boundaries
★ National capital

N
W—E
S

0   500   1,000 miles
0   500   1,000 kilometers

This map shows the extent of Mexico after it won its independence from Spain in 1821.

Finally, in 1821 a Spanish army officer named Agustín de Iturbide (ah goos TEEN de ee toor BEE day) joined the rebels. He had been accused of misusing army funds, and he thought he could do better with the rebels. So he brought his army unit into the war on the side of independence. That turned the tide in favor of the rebels. Iturbide led the revolutionary army into Mexico City on September 27, 1821, and declared Mexico a free and independent nation. After eleven years of fighting, the independence movement that had begun with Padre Hidalgo's "Cry of Dolores" had finally achieved its goal.

**A** **Marriage Ends in Tragedy** María Teresa was dying, and all Simón Bolívar could do was stand helplessly by and watch. She was the love of his life. He had met her just two years before, in 1801, while they were both living in Madrid, Spain.

They fell in love immediately and would have gotten married right away. But he was only 17, and her father insisted that they wait. Finally, she had become his wife. And now, less than a year after their marriage, she lay dying.

In some ways, Bolívar must have blamed himself for her death. As soon as they married, Bolívar had brought María Teresa back to Venezuela, where he had been born and owned property. Soon after, María Teresa caught yellow fever and died. If only he had stayed in Spain, he thought, it would not have happened.

But if Bolívar had stayed in Spain, and if María Teresa had not died, the history of South America would have been much different. He would not have become the most famous and successful **liberator** of South America.

> **vocabulary**
> **liberator** a person who frees a country from an enemy

At the time of María Teresa's death, Bolívar was only 20. He became restless and left Venezuela once more to travel in Europe. There, he lived for some time in France, where Napoleon now ruled. It was 1803. Bolívar read important Enlightenment writers like Montesquieu, Voltaire, and John Locke. His experiences in France and the rest of Europe convinced him that Venezuela must become independent. On a visit to Italy in 1805, Bolívar climbed to a religious shrine high above Rome. "I swear," Bolívar said, "by the God of my fathers and the honor of my country, I will not rest, not in body or soul, till I have broken the chains of Spain."

If María Teresa had lived, Bolívar might not have returned to Europe, and he almost certainly would not have devoted his life to fighting to liberate South America. "My wife's death," he later admitted, "led me early in my career onto the road of politics."

*Simón Bolívar is known throughout South America as "The Liberator."*

## Failed Rebellion

In 1807, Bolívar finally returned to Venezuela. He went back to the family hacienda and took up the life of a wealthy Creole farmer. However, Bolívar's quiet life would not last long; revolution was in the air, and he would be at the center of it.

But Bolívar was not the first Venezuelan to try to liberate the Spanish colony. In 1806, Francisco de Miranda, another Venezuelan, had tried to start a revolution against Spain. Miranda had traveled through the United States and Europe for years. He was a soldier and an adventurer. He had served in the armies of Spain and France. He had fought in the French Revolution and had become a general. He had traveled to the United States and met many leaders of the American Revolution—George Washington, Benjamin Franklin, Thomas Jefferson, and others. Miranda was convinced that Venezuela and the rest of Spain's American colonies should be free.

Miranda arrived in Venezuela in February 1806 with 150 men and a fleet of three ships, two of which he got in Santo Domingo and the third he got from the British navy. The Spanish authorities had been alerted and stopped him before he could land on Venezuelan soil. He lost two of the ships and 60 of his men.

Venezuelan independence was a lifelong dream for Miranda, however, and he refused to accept defeat. He went to Barbados, where the British gave him more ships and men. This time, Miranda landed his troops but found little local support. The Creoles, in particular, refused to rally behind him.

Miranda had spent a lifetime talking about independence, yet he failed now because he lacked support in his native land. The problem was that he had talked too much about equality. He had even suggested freeing the slaves. Most Creoles in Venezuela, as in Mexico, did not want equality. They enjoyed the power of being second only to the Spaniards and did not want their relationship with the lower classes changed. All the Creoles wanted was to get rid of the upper class, the Spaniards. To the Creoles, Miranda was a troublemaker who might ruin them all. And so,

unable to inspire these powerful Venezuelans with a zeal for independence, Miranda was driven off once more.

## The First Venezuelan Republic

Remember that in 1808, Napoleon overthrew the Spanish king and placed his brother Joseph on the Spanish throne. This meant that Venezuelans no longer had to worry about being disloyal to the true Spanish king if they pursued independence. By 1810 a group of Venezuelan Creoles was beginning to think Miranda was right about Venezuelan independence. Simón Bolívar became one of the leaders of these **conspirators**.

The conspirators first threw out the highest-ranking Spanish officer in the colony. He had been appointed by Napoleon's brother, Joseph. As a result, the conspirators could declare that they were acting out of loyalty to Ferdinand VII, the deposed Spanish king. Of course, they really intended to make Venezuela independent.

Bolívar was sent to get help from Great Britain. He failed to get any money, but he did convince Miranda to come back and lead the revolution. By this time, Miranda was 60, an advanced age for someone at this time. Miranda still believed in his dream of South American independence. Despite his age, he was also an able and experienced military leader. The would-be revolutionaries needed that experience to lead them in a fight against the Spanish army.

On July 5, 1811, the leaders of the rebellion declared Venezuela's independence and established what has become known as the First Republic.

But meanwhile, the Spanish forces in Venezuela were organizing. Also, many Venezuelan Creoles still opposed independence. Together, the Spanish troops and **royalists** fought back against the rebels. Royalists were people who supported the king and opposed independence.

**vocabulary**

**conspirator** someone who secretly plans an unlawful action, such as overthrowing the government

**royalist** someone who supports the rule of a king or queen

*The Venezuelan patriot, Francisco Miranda, is shown here signing Venezuela's Act of independence on July 5, 1811. Venezuela did not become completely free of Spanish rule until 1821.*

The revolutionary army gained important victories, but there was no overwhelming support for the new government. In addition, Bolívar and Miranda began to argue. Bolívar's supporters were Creoles. Miranda's strength came from the mestizos and Indians. The two men had different views. Most important, perhaps, they were both strong-willed and proud, and each wanted the glory and the power of being the leader. While the royalists gained strength, the quarrel between Miranda and Bolívar deepened.

The problems within the revolutionary movement were matched by uncertainty among the people. They were unsure of whom to support, the republicans or the royalists. Soon, an unexpected event gave them their answer.

## The Earth Shakes

March 26, 1812, was an extraordinarily hot day, even for steamy Venezuela. Except for a pattering of rain, all was unusually quiet. Suddenly, the earth began to shake violently. A low rumble broke the silence as houses and buildings cracked and then collapsed. The screams of trapped and injured people pierced the air.

A huge earthquake had struck Venezuela. Caracas and other areas under rebel control were the worst hit. Nearly 20,000 people were killed, including most of the rebel soldiers in Caracas. The capital and several other cities were nearly flattened, but the royalist-controlled towns were spared. The archbishop of Caracas, who was a royalist, preached that the earthquake was a message that God was on the side of the Spaniards. In the chaos that followed, the revolutionaries were defeated.

Miranda tried to negotiate with the Spanish authorities to let the rebels leave the country, but Bolívar and some of the other young officers claimed he was being disloyal. They turned him over to the Spaniards. Miranda died four years later in a Spanish prison. Meanwhile, the Spanish officials let Bolívar and his allies leave the country.

## War to the Death

Bolívar had to flee Venezuela, but he was not through fighting. He went to New Grenada, the colony next to Venezuela. Rebels in the capital, Bogotá (boh guh TAH), had declared independence in 1811. Bolívar joined the rebels of New Grenada. He was given command of a troop of soldiers at a place called Cúcuta (KOO koo tah), near the Venezuelan border. He defeated the Spanish garrisons there and won promotion to general in the rebel army.

Bolívar then convinced the leaders of New Grenada to let him lead an army to liberate Venezuela. He met little resistance at first, but soon the fighting became brutal. Spanish commanders often executed the rebels they captured. Finally, Bolívar proclaimed: "Those executioners who call themselves our enemies have broken international law. . . . But the victims will be avenged [and] these executioners exterminated. . . . Our hatred knows no bounds, and the war shall be to the death!"

The fight became bloodier. Both sides committed acts of terror and cruelty. But Bolívar's declaration of "war to the death" aided the rebels. Venezuelans could no longer remain undecided about the war around them. They had to decide, "Am I for independence or am I for Spain?" Those who failed to choose a side could be mistaken for the enemy. Many joined the revolution.

Bolívar continued his march through Venezuela. He won major battles and reached Caracas in three months. The pro-independence people of Venezuela regarded Bolívar as a hero. That's when people first began calling him "The Liberator."

Bolívar had earned a quick victory, but the war was far from over. And it became even bloodier and crueler than it had been.

The Andes form a high barrier on the western edge of South America bordering the Pacific Ocean. To the north lie vast plains called the Llanos (LYAH nohs). The Orinoco River, one of South America's largest rivers, flows through the Llanos.

The Llanos were divided into huge ranches. Cowboys, called llaneros (lyah NAY rohs), tended the cattle. These llaneros organized a formidable army that supported the royalists. They were master horsemen, armed with long lances with knives strapped to the end. Their leader, José Tomás Boves (hoh SAY toh MAHS BOH ves), was a Spaniard, and he may have been the most bloodthirsty and ruthless leader in any of the wars for independence.

Boves showed no mercy in war. Prisoners were automatically executed. In July 1814, Boves drove toward Caracas and forced Bolívar's troops to retreat back to New Grenada.

Things were not going well in New Grenada, either. The French had recently been driven from Spain, and King Ferdinand VII returned to the throne. Determined to restore his empire, Ferdinand sent an army of 11,000 men to regain control of Venezuela and New Grenada. It was the largest army Spain had ever sent to Latin America, and the rebels were

**New Grenada and Venezuela in the Early 1800s**

*The territory of New Grenada would become the modern countries of Panama, Colombia, and Ecuador.*

overwhelmed. The Spanish commander was ruthless in destroying the rebels and their leaders. Bolívar escaped to Haiti, which had been independent since 1804.

### Bolívar's Daring Plan

Bolívar was defeated, but he never gave up! He immediately began assembling a new army in Haiti, where he had the strong support of Pétion (pay TYAWN), the Haitian president. Pétion was an ex-slave, and he asked two things in exchange for his support. First, Bolívar must recognize Haiti's government once he set up a government in South America. Second, Bolívar must free all slaves. Bolívar agreed, and Pétion provided support that made the next stage in the independence movement possible.

Bolívar left Haiti with just 200 soldiers in seven small ships. He tried to land on the Venezuelan coast, but the effort failed. He needed the Venezuelans to join his army, but most either supported the royalists or were indifferent to the war altogether. Realizing that he could not succeed, Bolívar changed his strategy. By this time, the llaneros were unhappy with Spanish rule. If he could gain their support, Bolívar might still win the war.

In July 1817, Bolívar sailed up the Orinoco River and set up headquarters in the town of Angostura (ang guhs TOOR uh). It was a small and isolated town where the rebels could reorganize without interference from the Spaniards and royalists.

The plan worked. The llaneros now favored independence and joined Bolívar. In addition, more than 4,000 British **volunteers** joined the revolution. These troops were among the best in the rebel army. Now Bolívar was ready to try again to win independence for Venezuela and New Grenada.

### On to Bogotá!

Bolívar decided on a bold move: He would attack Bogotá, the capital of New Grenada. Bogotá was tucked safely away in the distant Andean highlands. The Spanish leaders thought no rebel army would be able to cross the hundreds of miles of trackless country and climb the mountains to attack such an isolated place. That's exactly why Bolívar did it.

In May 1819, Bolívar left Angostura, with 2,500 men. Crossing the Llanos was worse than facing the Spaniards. The army endured rain, wind, and floods. Clothing became mildewed. Saddles and boots fell apart. Even the hooves of the horses rotted. One soldier later recalled, "For seven days we marched in water up to our waists." Soldiers were swept away in floods, lost in quicksand, and killed by disease.

Matters got worse when they reached the mountains. All the horses died, and Bolívar lost many men. Hundreds died from exhaustion. The army abandoned everything but its guns. Even the artillery was left on the narrow, snow-covered and icy mountain trails. And still, the army struggled on until finally, exhausted and out of supplies, they descended from the mountains into New Grenada.

As Bolívar had hoped, his army surprised the Spanish troops. The battle of Boyacá (boi yuh KAH) was one of the most important in the entire **campaign**. The main Spanish army was beaten, and Bolívar marched into Bogotá almost without resistance. The people of Bogotá cheered Bolívar and welcomed him as a liberator. Bolívar left a general from New Grenada to set up a government there and then turned once again to the liberation of Venezuela.

Bolívar returned to Angostura where he joined forces with a new llanero chieftain, José Antonio Páez. The two of them led an army that met the royalists in the battle of Carababo. Once again, Bolívar surprised the royalist forces by attacking from an unexpected direction. The victory ended most of the Spanish resistance in Venezuela. Four days later, on June 28, 1821, Bolívar marched into Caracas. enezuela's independence had been won.

> **vocabulary**
> **volunteer** someone who chooses freely to do something, such as joining an army
> **campaign** a series of military operations

## Battles for Independence, 1817–1825

**Battles in South America**

- ⊗ (green) Battles led by Simon Bolívar
- ⊗ (red) Battles led by Antonio José de Sucre

*Caribbean Sea* · Santa Marta · Caracas · Cartagena · **Carabobo** · *Orinoco River* · **Cúcuta** · Angostura · Bogotá · **Boyacá** · 10°N

**Quito** · Guayaquil · *Amazon River* · 0° · ATLANTIC OCEAN · ANDES · 10°S · Lima · **Ayacucho** · Cuzco · **Upper Peru (Bolivia)** · MTS.

0  400  800 miles
0  400  800 kilometers

80°W · 70°W · 60°W · 50°W · 40°W

*Bolívar sent Sucre to fight the Spanish forces in Quito. The rebel victory liberated Ecuador.*

## Bolívar's Dream

After more than ten years of struggle, two battles had turned the tide, winning independence for New Grenada and Venezuela. With their independence, Bolívar was able to set in motion another dream for South America. He admired the United States. He was impressed that the 13 British colonies had united to form a single country. He dreamed of doing the same thing in South America. Uniting New Grenada and Venezuela was the beginning. The new country was called Gran Colombia. Its first constitution was written in 1821, and Bolívar became the first president. However, this was just the beginning.

Bolívar next turned his attention to the south. Lima, (LEE muh) Peru, had been the capital of Spanish South America for centuries, and it was a royalist stronghold. Capturing this city was a major objective on the road to independence for all of South America. But to get to Peru, the rebels would have to take the important city of Quito (KEE toh). Today, Quito is the capital of the country of Ecuador (EK wuh dor).

José Antonio Sucre (hoh SAY ahn TOH ny-oh SOO kray) was a native of Venezuela. He joined the revolution in 1810 and had followed Bolívar ever since. In 1821, Bolívar sent Sucre to Guayaquil (gwye ah KEEL), the main port city of Ecuador. There, he gathered an army to attack the Spanish forces in Quito.

Sucre's army met the Spanish forces on May 24, 1822. The Spanish were defeated, and Ecuador was liberated. Now only Peru remained to be liberated. However, another liberator was already there!

José de San Martín had been fighting since 1813 to liberate southern South America. By 1821, his army had reached Lima. Although San Martín declared independence for Peru, his army was not strong enough to beat the large Spanish forces that remained in mountain fortresses.

San Martín and Bolívar met in Guayaquil in July 1822. San Martín wanted Bolívar's help in liberating Peru. But the two great liberators were unable to come to an agreement. Neither was willing to give up power to the other. After the meeting in Guayaquil, San Martín took his army and marched to Chile.

Bolívar went to Lima in September 1823. However, something was different: The Peruvians did not trust him. He was a Venezuelan, and he was the president of Gran Colombia. No one in Lima wanted Peru to become a part of Gran Colombia.

Bolívar feared that, if he left the city to pursue the Spanish army, the people of Lima would turn against him. As a result, he asked Sucre to once again lead the army of liberation. Sucre's force met and defeated the Spanish army near the city of Ayacucho (ah yah KOO choh) on December 9, 1824. Peru was finally freed from Spanish rule.

With the liberation of Peru, only an area called Upper Peru remained under Spanish control. By this time, Bolívar believed that Lima was safely under his control. He handed over the command to Sucre, who freed upper Peru in 1825. This victory completed the liberation of South America. The leaders of Upper Peru wanted their homeland to become independent. They named the new country Bolivia (buh LIHV ee uh), in honor of Bolívar, the Liberator. He wrote a constitution for the country, and Sucre became its first president.

## The End of Bolívar's Dream

Bolívar had brought liberty to much of South America. But in his moment of triumph, things turned against him.

Following his victory in Bolivia, Bolívar returned to Lima and found the Peruvians plotting against him. Bolivia had already set itself up as an independent nation. Now Peru wanted to be independent as well. Back in Gran Colombia, conflicts were also arising. Bolívar hurried back to try to calm the storms that were raging there. He faced rebellions in Venezuela and unhappiness in Colombia. On top of all this, Bolívar was sick. He had tuberculosis. In those days, the disease was almost always fatal.

Bolívar proved to be a better general than he was a president. Bolívar's rule in Gran Colombia was dictatorial, and he was resented by many of his former supporters. Finally, in 1830, Gran Colombia broke up into the three countries of Venezuela, Colombia, and Ecuador. Bolívar's dream of a united South America had failed.

Bolívar, near death and discouraged, resigned as president and left Bogotá for the coastal city of Santa Marta. He planned to take a ship to Europe. When he got to Santa Marta, he found

*José Antonio Sucre and his army defeated the Spanish at the Battle of Ayacucho in 1824, freeing Peru from Spanish rule.*

out that his old friend General Sucre had been killed by political rivals. Bolívar was heartbroken. He canceled his trip and went to stay with a friend. He died there in December 1830.

At the end, when it was clear that South America would never be united, Bolívar was very discouraged. His reported last words show the sting of rejection he felt. "Let us go!" he whispered with his last breath. "Let us go!—the people do not want us in this land!"

**T**rouble in Buenos Aires Buenos Aires (BWAY nus EYE ress), Argentina, was a prosperous city and busy port in the early 1800s. Then, one morning in 1806, the residents of this Spanish city woke up to see ten large British warships anchored in their bay. You can imagine their surprise and their anxiety. What did this mean? What should they do?

They decided to wait to see what the Spanish **viceroy** would do. This official was appointed by the king of Spain to govern the colony. But he turned out to be a coward. As soon as he saw the British flags flying from the ships, he packed up and fled. Now, you can imagine how this made the citizens of Buenos Aires feel!

The British ships had in fact come to capture Buenos Aires. The British and Spaniards had been rivals and enemies for many years. The British had seized this moment to attempt to take this valuable colony away from Spain. The small Spanish army post was quickly overcome, and the British marched into the city.

The year was 1806. British troops stayed in Buenos Aires just long enough to steal the money from the treasury and send it back to Great Britain. Within two months, the people of the area organized a **militia** to resist the British invasion. The leader was Santiago de Liniers (sahn TYAH goh de lee NYERS), the commander of the Spanish fleet that had been away when the British came. The militia was an army made up largely of Creoles who lived near Buenos Aires. There were about 8,000 militia members along with 1,000 regular Spanish soldiers from Montevideo. Montevideo is on the opposite side of the Río (River) de la Plata from Buenos Aires and is today the capital of Uruguay.

> **vocabulary**
> **viceroy** a ruler of a colony or territory
> **militia** an army made up of civilians rather than professional soldiers

*Buenos Aires, Argentina, as it looks today.*

The militia soon drove off the British troops and the fleet. The cabildo, or city council, of Buenos Aires then refused to let the old viceroy have his position back. Instead, they elected Santiago de Liniers as the new viceroy. This was a revolutionary act, because only the king had the right to appoint a viceroy.

Soon Great Britain sent a larger fleet with 12,000 men to retake the city. This time, the citizens were ready. They fought bravely and defeated the larger and better-trained British force. Everyone helped to drive off the enemy. Even those who could not fight helped out by bringing food and water to the men who were fighting and by tending the wounds of those injured in battle.

After the British sailed off, the citizens of Buenos Aires began wondering why they needed the Spanish government at all. Hadn't they defended themselves? Couldn't they govern themselves?

In recognition of his success in defending Buenos Aires, the Spanish king made Santiago de Liniers the temporary viceroy. Liniers understood how important trade was to the people of Buenos Aires. He allowed British ships to come into the port and trade. People began to make money, and everyone was happy. But Liniers was only the temporary viceroy. After a few months the king sent a permanent viceroy. The new viceroy began enforcing the old trade rules. Now the British ships couldn't trade legally. People made less money and had less to spend.

## Independence in La Plata

As you know, events in Europe had a big effect on the politics of the South American colonies beginning in 1810. By that time, Napoleon Bonaparte had conquered Spain and replaced the king with his brother Joseph Bonaparte. The people of Buenos Aires were unhappy with the new viceroy and his policies, and now they had lost their king. They met to decide what to do.

A Creole lawyer named Mariano Moreno (mah RYAH noh  moh RAY noh) became a leader of the cabildo. He was a man of great energy who had the courage to voice his opinions. He convinced the city council to remove the king's

viceroy and send him into exile. Moreno and the cabildo wanted La Plata to be independent. La Plata included the area that now is the countries of Argentina, Uruguay, Paraguay, and Bolivia. Buenos Aires was the capital of La Plata. The people of Buenos Aires knew they could run their own affairs after having twice defeated the British invasion forces. The strong leadership of Mariano Moreno also helped.

Moreno died in 1811. La Plata still was not independent, but the cabildo of Buenos Aires ruled without interference from Spain. However, people in other parts of La Plata began to worry about being dominated by the capital. Uruguay and Paraguay had local leaders who refused to accept the rule of Buenos Aires. Upper Peru, which would become Bolivia, was still under Spanish rule. Other provinces were also uneasy and threatened to set up their own government. Buenos Aires was busy trying to keep them under its control.

## José de San Martín Returns

José de San Martín would become the main leader of the revolutions in southern South America. San Martín, a Creole, was especially suited to his role. He was born to Spanish parents in a small town about 500 miles north of Buenos Aires. His father was a soldier and an administrator on the La Plata frontier. When San Martín was six years old, his father took his family back to Spain.

San Martín went to school in Spain and became an officer in the Spanish army. He was a loyal and capable officer. He fought in several wars, including the war against France when Napoleon invaded Spain. Then, in 1811 he retired from the army, and the next year he returned to La Plata.

This must have been a difficult decision for San Martín. He was at the height of his career as a military officer. He was needed by both Spain and his king; and he had always shown great loyalty to both. Somehow, though, he decided to turn his back on all of this. Many years later, San Martín explained that he gave up his career because La Plata needed him. He had not been there since he was six years old, but it drew him like a magnet.

After leaving the Spanish army, San Martín went to London. There, he met Francisco de Miranda and other revolutionaries. You may remember that Miranda had also been a soldier. The two men must have compared their experiences fighting in different wars. No other Latin American revolutionary leaders had as much military experience as they did. Then, in January 1812, San Martín left for South America.

In September of that year, San Martín married María de los Remedios (mah REE ah de lohs re MEH dee ohs), the young daughter of a Spanish merchant in Buenos Aires. Although newly married, San Martín would spend most of the next ten years away from home.

María de los Remedios's new husband and the other revolutionaries faced many problems. The leaders in Buenos Aires had hoped to go through Upper Peru to get to Lima, Peru, the capital of Spanish power in South America. But Spain had large armies in those colonies, so freedom would not be easy to win. Chile had declared independence in 1810, but Spain had defeated the rebels and held power in the capital, Santiago.

San Martín argued that La Plata's troops should liberate Chile first. Then they could go by sea to Lima. This would be better than attacking Upper Peru and facing the strong Spanish force there. Since San Martín had more military experience than any of the other leaders, they followed his advice.

José de San Martín was the principal leader of the revolts against Spain in the southern parts of South America.

## Independence Comes to Chile

San Martín planned his campaign carefully. It started with a trick: He pretended to be sick. That was his excuse for being sent as governor to the province of Cuyo (KOO yoh). It appeared to be a restful job where he could recover his health. Actually, Cuyo shared a border with Chile and was a key to the routes through the Andes. San Martín spent two years in the province getting troops ready to invade Chile. He thought he could surprise the Spanish army by going over the highest part of the mountains. No one would expect an attack from there.

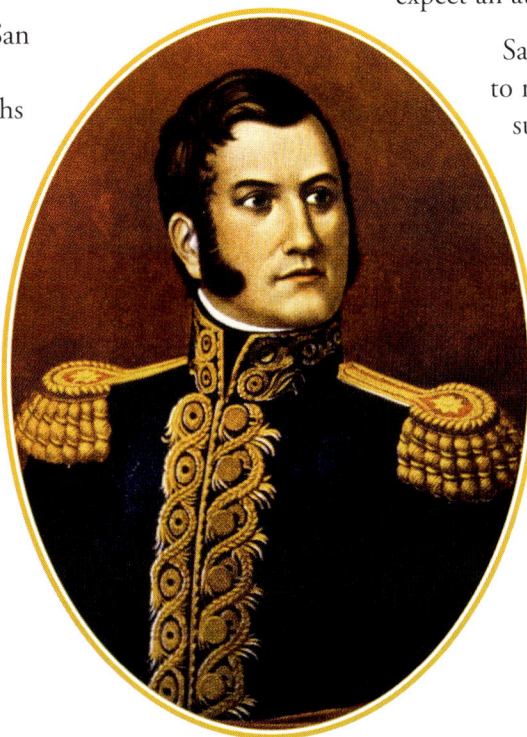

San Martín worked hard to make sure his plan would succeed. He sent spies to Chile to find out where the Spanish army camps were and how many soldiers they had. In addition to finding out about the Spanish army, the spies planted false rumors about possible rebellions and encouraged support from Chilean patriots.

Then San Martín did the cleverest thing of all. He invited a group of Pehuenche (pay WEN chay) Indians, who lived near a low pass in the Andes, to a meeting. He gave the Indians gifts and asked for permission to cross their territory into Chile. This would have been the easiest way to go over the Andes. After all the secrets, why did San Martín act so openly? Because the clever general knew the Indians would tell the Spanish officials about the meeting. This would make the Spaniards expect an invasion from the south. But San Martín had other ideas. He would cross the Andes over the highest pass and attack from the east.

Finally, on January 18, 1817, San Martín's army left Mendoza (men DOH zuh), the capital of Cuyo. He had with him nearly 4,000 soldiers and 1,000 men to carry ammunition and food. In addition, they had 10,600 mules, 1,600 horses, and 700 head of cattle. Cannons were carried in pieces on carts, but they actually had to be hauled by hand much of the way. What these troops did ranks as one of the great military accomplishments in history.

San Martín's army crossed the Andes in the shadow of 22,800 foot-high Mount Aconcagua (ak un KAHG wuh), the highest mountain in the Americas. They passed through narrow canyons, along sheer bluffs, and through passes that were 12,000 feet above sea level. By the time the army reached Chile, on the western side of the mountains, they had only 4,300 mules and 511 horses left, and all were in bad shape. Nevertheless, San Martín's army had crossed the Andes in only 21 days. And they were well armed and had enough supplies to press the attack.

The daring gamble paid off. The Spanish leaders knew an attack was coming, but they weren't sure where it would be. They divided up their army to cover different routes. But they never expected an army could cross the Andes as San Martín's forces did. San Martín surprised

and defeated a large Spanish army in a battle south of Santiago near a place called Chacabuco. San Martín's army captured 600 Spanish soldiers along with all their artillery and supplies.

The road to Santiago was open, and San Martín marched into the city, along with Bernardo O'Higgins, a Chilean who had commanded a division in the battle of Chacabuco. O'Higgins was named governor of Chile. Spanish resistance continued for more than a year, with O'Higgins and San Martín leading the Chilean forces. Chile declared its independence on February 12, 1818, but fighting continued for another two months before the last Spanish troops were defeated.

### Failure in Peru

Now, San Martín faced his greatest challenge. The way was clear for an attack on Peru, where Spain had its strongest forces. San Martín assembled a fleet. In August 1820, he sailed to southern Peru with an army of more than 4,000. Awaiting him was a Spanish army of 23,000 men. San Martín knew he couldn't defeat the larger Spanish force in battle. He hoped the Peruvians would rise up against Spain and that Spanish troops would desert. In fact, some Spanish soldiers did desert,

*San Martín reviews his troops before fighting the Spanish in Chile.*

*On August 20, 1820, San Martín and his forces arrived in Peru.*

but the Peruvians did not rise up in rebellion. Still, San Martín was able to move his army to Lima.

With the protection of San Martín's army, Peru declared independence on July 28, 1821. San Martín could protect Lima, but he knew his army wasn't strong enough to defeat the Spanish forces elsewhere in the country. But all was not yet lost to San Martín. As you know, Simón Bolívar was at the same time hoping to liberate Peru. San Martín sailed to Guayaquil in July 1822 to meet with Bolívar. He hoped that together they could defeat the Spanish and bring independence to Peru.

You know, however, that the meeting did not go as San Martín had hoped. San Martín left Guayaquil a disappointed man. He immediately returned to Lima, resigned as the city's protector, and took his army back to Chile. Bolívar and José Antonio Sucre completed the struggle for Peruvian independence.

San Martín went back to Mendoza, where he had a small farm. There, news of yet another tragedy reached him. He learned in 1823 that his wife had died in Buenos Aires. He returned to that city, but his enemies controlled the government. San Martín knew he could have no role in the new government, so he took his young daughter and sailed for Europe.

San Martín had gained nothing from his years of work. He had no money. The countries he freed didn't even offer him a **pension** until long after he had left. He visited France and Great Britain and lived for several years in Brussels, Belgium. In 1838 he moved to a small town in France where he died in 1850.

San Martín, like Bolívar, had hoped to unite all of Spain's South American provinces. In the end, neither of the great heroes of independence realized this dream.

### vocabulary

**pension** money that is not a salary that is paid regularly to a person who has performed some service or work

**A** **Ruler's New Home** Never had a European ruler set foot in America until João (zhwoun), prince of Portugal, did at the beginning of the nineteenth century, when he came to Brazil. Moreover, João had not come to Brazil just for a visit. He had come to make it his home and the capital of the Portuguese empire.

Why was João moving permanently to Brazil? Like much that happened throughout Latin America during this period, this action was set in motion by Napoleon. Portugal is a small country in Europe. Traditionally, it had a close **alliance** with Great Britain. But when Napoleon was marching through Spain, he demanded that Portugal, neighbor to Spain, break those ties with Britain. João was told that he must close his ports to British ships, take away all property belonging to British citizens, and arrest all British citizens. Now, João, like all monarchs, was very proud. He didn't like taking orders from Napoleon. He may also have believed that in the long run, Great Britain was a better and more powerful friend than Napoleon. In any case, João did close his ports to British ships, but he refused to do more.

> **vocabulary**
> **alliance** a group of countries that join together to accomplish some goal

As you can probably guess, Napoleon wasn't satisfied, so he invaded Portugal. João had already considered the possibility of moving his capital to Brazil. So the very day that Napoleon's troops entered his capital of Lisbon, Portugal, João boarded a British ship and set out for South America.

It took a fleet of 36 ships to hold all the royal treasures—jewels, important papers, books, paintings and statues, and thousands of other things. Along with the royal treasure came more than 10,000 people. These were the nobles, counts, barons, and lords of the court, along with their family members, servants, and helpers. The fleet was escorted by British warships to protect it from Napoleon's navy.

The voyage was terrible. The ships were filled with rats, fleas, and lice. The quarters were cramped and smelly. It was made even worse because the ships were crowded. Some of them carried three times as many people as they were intended for. The voyage in lumbering sailing ships took nearly two months.

To make matters worse, a storm struck the fleet, and some ships became separated. The destination had been Rio de Janeiro (REE oh dee zhuh NER oh), the capital of Brazil. Because of the rough voyage, many of the ships, including the king's, stopped first in Salvador da Bahia, the capital of a northern province of Brazil. As you can imagine, the visit came as a complete surprise to the townspeople.

### In Bahia

Bahia had no paved streets. There were no hotels or places fit for a king and nobles to stay. The royal family and all the members of the court had to stay in the houses of the citizens of Bahia. João's wife, Carlota, got lice on board the ship, so they had to shave off all her hair. She was furious. From that time on, she hated Brazil.

Although João did not linger long in Bahia, he already began acting as though Brazil was home. Soon after his arrival, he was visited by the governor of Bahia. The governor asked João to open Brazil's ports to international trade. For the past 300 years, Portugal had kept a tight rein on the trade of its colonies. Now, João had a new view of matters. He could see that restricting the trade of the colony was bad for the economy and the people. He immediately opened the ports to all nations. The change had a rapid effect on Brazil. During the following three years, Bahia alone increased its **exports** by 15 percent and its **imports** by 50 percent.

## Rio Becomes an Imperial City

After the brief stop in Bahia, João and his court traveled on to Rio de Janeiro. João made this city into the capital of the Portuguese empire. All the provinces of Brazil, along with the Portuguese colonies in Africa and Asia, were ruled from Rio. The taxes from this vast empire now streamed into Rio. People from all over Europe arrived to be near the Portuguese court and to do business with the empire. More than 24,000 Portuguese, along with many French and English people, arrived in Rio. Within ten years the population of the city doubled.

> **vocabulary**
> **export** something that is sent out of a country
> **import** something that is brought into a country

There was a lot of work to be done to make the city look worthy of the Portuguese empire.

João ordered that buildings be built for the treasures he had brought from Portugal—a library, an art museum, an institute of natural history. In addition, a naval and a military academy, a medical school, and an academy of fine arts were established. Primary and secondary schools were encouraged. Printing presses began operating, and new newspapers were established.

João also helped the Brazilian economy. In addition to opening the ports to world trade, he encouraged Brazilians to develop industry and agriculture.

Brazilians soon learned that there were other changes in store for them. Because it was the center of the empire, many government offices were established. There was the Council of State, the Treasury Council, and many others. The people of Rio became familiar with government structure. They found that it was much easier than before to get the government to listen to them and to hear what they needed. On the other hand, they also found that their activities were under close observation.

At first, many of the people in João's court may have believed their stay in Brazil was temporary. Surely, they must have thought, we'll return to

*This nineteenth-century painting of Rio de Janeiro's harbor shows Rio around the time that it became the capital of the Portuguese Empire.*

Europe as soon as Napoleon is gone from Portugal. They were wrong. Napoleon, in fact, was forced to withdraw from Portugal by the end of 1808, just months after his invasion. By that time, João had already learned to love Rio and Brazil. He had no intention of leaving. Years passed. In Portugal, people wondered why João was delaying his return.

In 1815, Napoleon's hold on Europe came to a final end in his defeat at Waterloo. His threat to Europe was over for good. And still, João and his court remained happily in Rio. To help justify his stay in Brazil, João changed the name of his empire. It became the United Kingdom of Portugal and Brazil. Now, Brazil was the equal of Portugal, and João continued to rule his empire from Rio.

For the people of Brazil, this new title gave them a sense of pride. It fed their desire for independence.

## Brazil Becomes an Empire

João prolonged his stay in Brazil. He loved Rio de Janeiro and probably could have been happy staying there forever. But Portugal was itself undergoing a revolution. Leaders of the revolution wanted to write a new constitution and limit the power of the monarch. They demanded João's return. If he didn't go back, he might lose his crown. So, in 1821, João reluctantly took his court and sailed for Portugal. João's son Pedro stayed behind in Brazil to rule in his place.

Meanwhile, Brazilians knew all about the revolutions that had been occurring in the Spanish

*Pedro I , the son of King João of Portugal, ruled Brazil from 1821 to 1831.*

colonies. Some of Brazil's leaders wanted to make their colony free, too. King João knew this when he left, and he warned his son, "If Brazil demands independence, proclaim it yourself and put the crown on your own head."

Portugal's revolutionary leaders worried that Pedro would declare Brazil independent. They wanted him to come to Portugal, too. Pedro was staying near São Paulo (soun POU loo) when the order came to return to Portugal. Instead, Pedro followed his father's advice. He tore the Portuguese flag off his uniform and declared "Independence or death!" A small Portuguese army post at Bahia tried to defend the colony for Portugal, but the Brazilians soon overwhelmed it. Brazil was independent in a nearly bloodless revolution.

Pedro I, as he came to be known, declared himself emperor of Brazil. The country had become an empire. Brazil is a huge country, and there was a danger that it would break up into several smaller independent countries as the former Spanish colonies had done. Pedro I managed to keep that from happening. The country did not break up, and Pedro and his son ruled Brazil for more than 65 years. Finally, in 1889, Pedro I's son, Pedro II, was forced to give up his crown, and Brazil became a **republic**.

> **vocabulary**
> **republic** a nation without a king, where elected officials govern

**W**hat Independence Didn't Do By 1830, most of the nations of Latin America had won their independence. The Haitians had driven out the French, and the Mexicans had expelled the Spanish. Bolívar and San Martín had liberated Spanish-speaking South America, and Pedro I had broken with his native Portugal to rule an independent Brazil.

However, independence did not solve all of the problems facing the people of Latin America. For one thing, independence did not bring unity. Both Bolívar and San Martín had hoped that the various colonies in South America would combine under a single federal government, like the states in the United States. But that didn't happen. South America split up into a number of independent countries.

The same thing happened in Central America. The colonies of Guatemala, Honduras, El Salvador, Nicaragua, and Costa Rica became independent in 1821, along with Mexico. At first these colonies became part of Mexico. Within two years, however, they declared their independence a second time and formed a country of their own called the United Provinces of Central America. Once again, the idea was to form a group of states on the model of the United States. But once again the plan failed. The provinces became independent nations between 1838 and 1840.

Independence also proved easier to achieve than stability. Many of the newly independent countries in South and Central America had trouble establishing stable, trustworthy governments to replace the Spanish colonial government. In many countries, strongmen known as **caudillos** (kaw DEE yohz) competed for power. The caudillos would fight among themselves until a clear victor emerged. Each caudillo would rule until someone else became powerful enough to replace him.

Class issues also persisted. Remember how Creoles throughout Latin America felt that they were treated unfairly by Spanish-born rulers? Well, when the Spanish were defeated, the Creoles ended up running many of the new Latin American countries. But not much else changed. The Creoles often refused to treat the mestizos and Indians as equals. So independence by itself did not necessarily ensure justice or political equality.

> **vocabulary**
> **caudillo** a military dictator in Latin American countries

## Mexico's Violent History

Mexico provides a good example of the difficulties that many Latin American countries encountered after gaining independence. In Lesson 3 you read about how Agustín de Iturbide and his soldiers completed the work begun by Padre Hidalgo and continued by José María Morelos. It was Iturbide who finally enabled Mexico to secure its independence in 1821.

Unfortunately, Iturbide's victory led to a new set of problems. Iturbide turned out to be very ambitious. He had himself declared emperor of Mexico, and he appointed his friends as counts and lords. The emperor's friends got fancy uniforms and spent the country's money freely. Bribery and corruption became common practices.

Then things went from bad to worse. The country ran out of money, and Iturbide was overthrown and sent out of Mexico. He was told he would be shot if he ever came back. Nevertheless, he did come back, hoping to regain power. He was captured and shot in 1824.

After the execution of Iturbide, the Creoles took over the government. They tried to make Mexico a republic and adopted a constitution partly based on the U.S. Constitution. This constitution sounded good on paper, but it didn't work too well in practice.

One problem was that the Mexicans had gotten rid of the Spaniards but had not gotten rid of the old Spanish class system. The Creoles had replaced the Spaniards at the top, but the mestizos and Indians were treated just as badly as before. Many slaved away on the haciendas, and few had any land of their own. To members of these lower classes it seemed that the revolution was only half complete: It had brought them independence but not justice or equal rights.

### General Santa Anna

Another problem was that the government the Creoles created lacked stability and was vulnerable to military takeovers by caudillos. Over the next few decades Mexico ran through a whole series of strongmen. The most notorious and most persistent of these strongmen was General Antonio López de Santa Anna. Santa Anna was president or virtual ruler of Mexico eleven different times during a span of 30 years. Each time the opposition ran him out of power, he would find a way to get back in.

Santa Anna was a proud man who was always commissioning statues of himself. He wore elaborate uniforms and forced the Mexican people to address him as "Your Most Serene Highness." Santa Anna was also a dishonest, unprincipled man who used his position to fill his own pockets.

During one of Santa Anna's several stints as ruler of Mexico, American settlers in Texas rebelled against the Mexican government and demanded independence. Santa Anna decided he would crush the rebellious Texans. In 1836, he led an army of 4,000 against a small Texan force holed up in the Alamo, a mission in San Antonio, Texas. Santa Anna won the battle but lost the war. The Texans, inspired by their battle cry, "Remember the Alamo!" eventually defeated Santa Anna and gained their independence.

A decade later Santa Anna lost another war, this time with the United States. By the end of the Mexican-American War of 1846-1848, Mexico had lost roughly half of its territory to the United States. It gave up California, New Mexico, Arizona, and parts of several other southwestern states. These losses weakened Santa Anna, and he was overthrown for the last time in 1855.

*The Alamo as it looks today.*

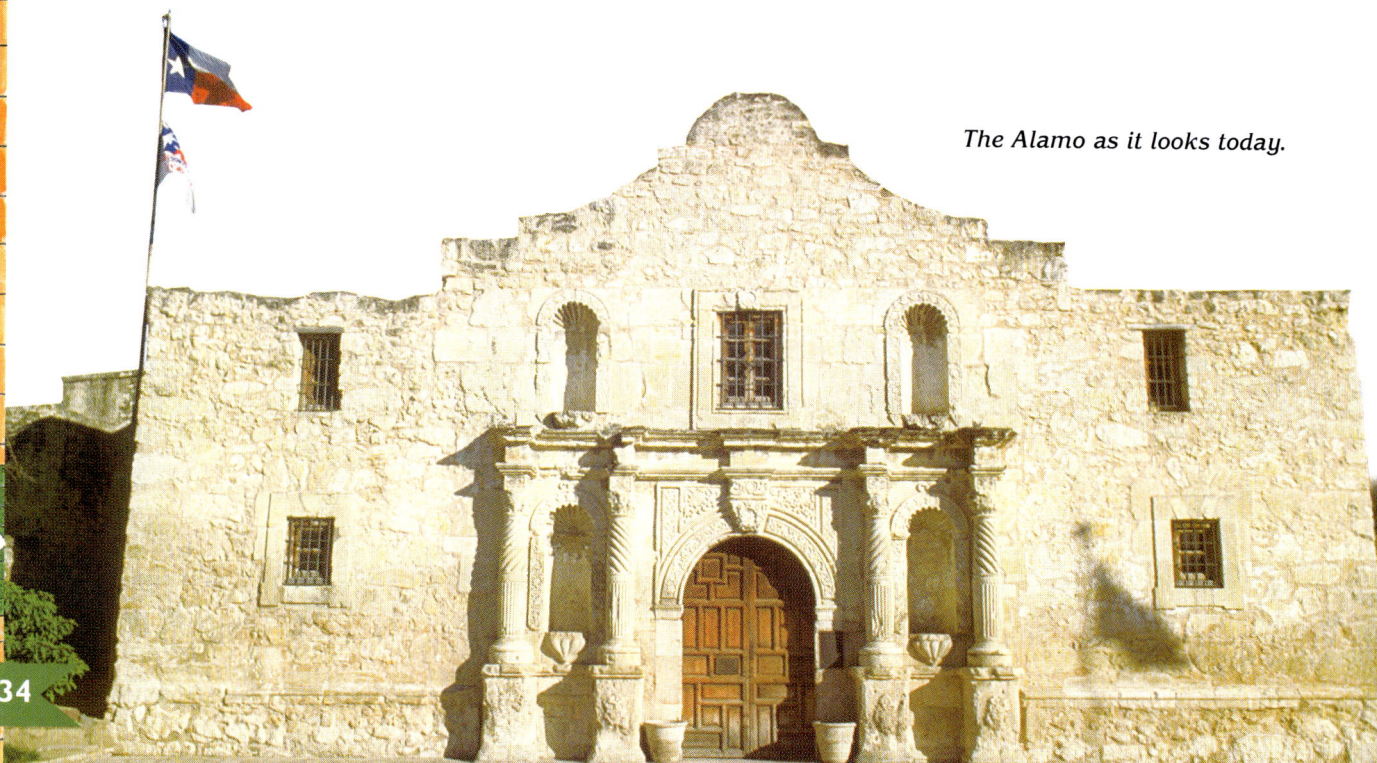

## Benito Juárez

Benito Juárez (be NEE toh HWAH res), an Indian lawyer from southeast Mexico, was the minister of justice in the government that followed Santa Anna's expulsion. Juárez had opposed Santa Anna for many years and was about as different from Santa Anna as could be imagined. Juárez came from a poor family and always wore a plain black suit. He was famous for his honesty and sympathy for the poor and for his belief in democracy and freedom of speech.

*After three years of ineffectual rule, Maximilian was executed by firing squad.*

As minister of justice, Juárez led a sweeping political reform movement designed to guarantee equal rights for all Mexicans. He also helped create Mexico's constitution of 1857. The following year Juárez became president, according to the provisions of the new constitution. As President, Juárez continued to work for reform. But powerful opposition to his reforms soon forced him to leave Mexico City.

Three years of fighting ensued. By late 1860 the opposition was defeated, and Juárez could return to the capital city. At that time, Mexico faced extreme financial difficulties. Constant wars had left the country deeply in debt to France, Spain, and Great Britain. Juárez decided to stop payments on the debt. Of course, these countries were not happy about his decision, and in 1862 they sent troops to Mexico. The British and Spaniards soon left, but the French remained. Napoleon III, the ruler of France, now ordered his troops to conquer Mexico.

## Cinco de Mayo

French troops marched on Mexico City. On May 5, 1862, a small Mexican force won a glorious victory over a much larger French army near the city of Puebla. Today, that victory is celebrated as a national holiday called Cinco de Mayo (SEENG koh de MAH yoh), or the Fifth of May. It is one of Mexico's most festive holidays.

Unfortunately, this great victory was not enough to keep the French from occupying Mexico City. As the French army closed in on the Mexican capital, Juárez sadly prepared to leave once again. He kissed the Mexican flag and shouted to a cheering crowd, *"Viva México!"* He fled to the north and spent the next few years traveling through the countryside, eluding capture and rallying the support of the Mexican people.

In 1864, Napoleon III named a young Austrian prince, Maximilian, emperor of Mexico. French troops kept Maximilian in power for three years, but when Napoleon called his troops home, Maximilian could no longer hold off the supporters of Juárez. Maximilian was soon captured, convicted of treason, and executed by a firing squad. Mexico's constitutional government was restored, and Juárez was once again reinstated as president.

Juárez worked hard to rebuild a country weakened by civil wars and foreign invasions. His government built schools and roads and did what it could to improve the lives of the poor. Juárez died in 1872. Today, he is honored as a great lawmaker and patriot, and as the man who saved Mexico's independence.

You might think that the triumph of Juárez would signal the end of Mexico's troubles. Unfortunately, it didn't. After Juárez died, Mexico fell into the hands of yet another caudillo, Porfirio Díaz. Díaz ruled Mexico, with one brief intermission, from 1876 until 1911. He modernized Mexico by building railroads, mines, and factories. Modernization was certainly needed, but foreigners and wealthy Mexicans benefited more from Díaz's modernizing programs than the poor. During Diaz's reign, a single Mexican family owned more than seven million acres of land, and the American newspaper baron William Randolph Hearst had a Mexican ranch as large as Delaware and Maryland put together. But the Indians, whose situation had begun to improve under Juárez, sank back into poverty. The vast majority still lacked both land and the political rights they had hoped independence would bring.

In the 1910s another wave of revolutions swept through Mexico. The revolutionaries wanted to "complete" the revolution that had begun way back in 1810 and push beyond the reforms of Juárez by obtaining land and rights for Indians. Two figures who played crucial roles in these revolutions were the guerrilla leaders Pancho Villa (PAHN cho VEE yah) and Emiliano Zapata (zah PAH tah).

### Pancho Villa

Pancho Villa was a cattle rustler and bandit who eventually joined the revolution against Díaz. He was a violent man but also very brave, and his followers were passionately devoted to him. Villa and his bandits won military victories in northern Mexico that helped the revolution topple Díaz from power. But Villa quickly lost his faith in the new government, which he believed had betrayed the cause of the poor people. So Villa became an outlaw and waged war on the new government, just as he had waged war on the old one.

Villa's great military success was due to his outstanding knowledge of the land and his use of guerrilla tactics. Rather than fight like regular soldiers, Villa and his men would stage lightning raids and then disappear into the hills.

*The Mexican revolutionary Pancho Villa crossed the Rio Grande twice and raided two American towns.*

When the United States backed the government Villa opposed, Villa staged a raid across the border. In 1916 he and his troops killed sixteen Americans in Columbus, New Mexico. United States President Woodrow Wilson sent a search expedition to find and capture Villa. But the clever Villa eluded the army scouts who had been sent to find him. Villa's knowledge of the land and his ability to disappear into the night helped him avoid capture.

## Emiliano Zapata

Emiliano Zapata was a guerrilla leader from the south of Mexico. Zapata was a mestizo who also joined the revolution against Díaz. Early in the struggle, Zapata called for the revolutionary government to take land from the wealthy landowners and give it to poor landless Indians. The heritage of the haciendas was still alive in Mexico. Wealthy landowners controlled almost all the land. Poor Mexicans had no lands and could earn their living only by working for the wealthy landowners under very difficult conditions.

Like Villa, Zapata was a first-rate guerrilla leader. He rallied people to his cause and assembled an effective fighting force. Like Villa, Zapata fought for the revolution and then fought against it when he concluded that the new revolutionary government had no intention of giving land to the Indians.

There was one leader who did support Zapata's plan; it was Pancho Villa. He and Zapata teamed up, promising to fight together until a government that was supportive of the plan was established.

During this time, Zapata's power grew until it extended throughout southern Mexico. Zapata and Villa's armies were strong enough to march into and occupy Mexico City in 1914. But they were not strong enough to take and hold on to power. Villa retreated to the north and Zapata to the south, where they continued to fight government forces.

Villa and Zapata had the successes they did because they fought for the causes of poor people —land, freedom, and justice. Indians, Mestizos, and freedom-loving Mexicans saw them as fighting for the same things that had led Padre Hidalgo to start Mexico's first revolution more than a century earlier.

Like Villa, Zapata was disappointed when the United States supported the Mexican government he was opposing. Zapata wanted people to know of the justness of the cause he was fighting for. That was why he was cheered by an article written by a United States official who had visited southern Mexico and had seen the Zapatistas (followers of Zapata) with his own eyes. The American wrote that compared with the disorganization of the Mexican national government, "the true social revolution [could] be found only among the Zapatistas." When Zapata read these articles, he declared, "Now I can die in peace. Finally, they have done us justice."

Shortly afterward, Zapata was tricked into meeting with the leaders of the army on the other side. The soldiers misled Zapata into thinking that they would join him and support his reforms. Instead, they ambushed him at a hacienda in southern Mexico and killed him. However, Zapata had accomplished much. He had created farm commissions to distribute land to the people and established Mexico's first agricultural credit bank. His enemies regarded him as a pillaging bandit, but the Indians hailed him as a revolutionary reformer and hero.

## Toward Equality

By 1920 a new government managed to establish law and order. But the costs of the Mexican Revolution of 1910–20 had been staggering. As many as 2 million Mexicans had died in the fighting. The Mexican Revolution is still the deadliest war ever fought on the American continent—more deadly even than the American Civil War.

The new government sought to heal the wounds caused by a decade of war. It convinced Pancho Villa to retire from revolutionary activity and settle on a ranch in northern Mexico. But Villa's enemies did not forget him. In 1923 he was shot to death by some of his political opponents.

Neither Villa nor Zapata lived to see all of their political wishes fulfilled, but they did help move Mexico closer to the goals of equality and justice for all. And the fame of the two outlaw guerrillas continues to this day. Both Villa and Zapata have been celebrated in countless stories, legends, movies, and songs.

## Latin American Dreams and Realities

By the middle of the twentieth century, Mexico finally settled down and made great progress towards democracy and justice. But other Latin American countries continued to wrestle with the same problems. Indeed, almost every country in Latin America has experienced the same cycle of caudillos, revolution, civil war, and violence.

Yet these nations also have another past—a past brightened by the accomplishments of Toussaint L'Ouverture, Miguel de Hidalgo y Costilla, Simón Bolívar, José de San Martín, and Bernardo O'Higgins. These men started with noble dreams of freedom and independence and worked to turn those ideas into realities. Their accomplishments remain inspiring today.

*Emiliano Zapata (standing) is shown here holding the slogan of his revolutionary movement. The slogan reads, "Tierra y Libertad"— "Land and Liberty." The artist is Diego Rivera.*

**alliance** a group of countries that join together to accomplish some goal

**cabildo** the government of a city in Latin America; the city council

**campaign** a series of military operations

**caudillo** a military dictator in Latin American countries

**conspirator** someone who secretly plans an unlawful action, such as overthrowing the government

**export** something that is sent out of a country

**guerrilla army** a group of soldiers who usually are volunteers and not highly trained, professional soldiers

**hacienda** a large ranch or plantation in Latin America

**import** something that is brought into a country

**liberator** a person who frees a country from an enemy

**machete** a large, heavy knife used for cutting down sugarcane and brush

**militia** an army made up of civilians rather than professional soldiers

**mural** a large picture that is usually painted directly on the wall of a building

**padre** the Spanish word for "father"; a traditional form of address for a Roman Catholic priest

**pension** money that is not a salary that is paid regularly to a person who has performed some service or work

**plantation** a large farm

**republic** a nation without a king, where elected officials govern

**royalist** someone who supports the rule of a king or queen

**scythe** a long, curving blade used for cutting grain and long grasses

**viceroy** a ruler of a colony or territory

**volunteer** someone who chooses freely to do something, such as joining an army

# CREDITS

All photographs © Pearson Learning unless otherwise noted.

**PHOTOS:**
**Cover:**
*bkgd.* Ken Welsh/The Bridgeman Art Library; *frgd.* SuperStock.
**Interior:**
1: Sean Sprague/Mexicolore/The Bridgeman Art Library, London/SuperStock, Inc.
5: J. P. Zenobel/The Bridgeman Art Library. 6: Michael Holdford. 7: The Granger Collection, New York.
8–9: Bettmann/Corbis. 10: Musee National du Chateau de Malmaison, Rueil-Malmaison/
Lauros-Giraudon/SuperStock, Inc. 11: The Bridgeman Art Library. 13: Culver Pictures, Inc.
15: The Granger Collection, New York. 16: Culver Pictures, Inc. 18: Explorer, Paris/SuperStock, Inc.
20: The Granger Collection, Inc. 25: SuperStock, Inc. 27: The Granger Collection, New York.
28: Index/The Bridgeman Art Library. 29: Instituto Sanmartino, Buenos Aires, Argentina/Index/
The Bridgeman Art Library. 31: The Bridgeman Art Library. 32: The Granger Collection, New York. 34:
Bob Daemmrich/PictureQuest. 35: Culver Pictures, Inc. 36: The Granger Collection, New York.
38: Art Resource.

**Maps:**
4, 17, 21, 23: Mapping Specialists, Ltd.

**Border Art:**
Michael Storrings/Artville/PictureQuest.